Deadly Survival Gear:

Learn Most Popular Mistakes That Will Kill You While Surviving

Table of Contents

Introduction

Welcome to Mistakes That Survivalists Can Make And How They Can Lead To Troubled situations, a D.I.Y. book about the common mistakes that survivalists make and how you can both avoid them and fix ones you might have made. This book is about surviving in the wilderness rather than prepping for survival. As with many survivalists books, I assume that you have been put into the situation rather than volunteering to be in that situation. Let's begin.

Chapter 1 – Where are you going?

The very first mistake you could make is often the one you feel that sometimes you have no choice over. I am assuming this book will be used for survival and not the thrill for survival, just to make things clear before we begin. This means that once you are put into a situation in which you need to survive until you reach your destination, there is one crucial *compounded* mistake that you could make that could end in your death and that is choosing where to go.

The Problem of Choosing where to Go?

A lot, and I mean a lot, of people choose the "go nowhere" method above all else. You are dropped in a forest or you are in a city full of chaos and *nothing* seems like the best option until you figure out everything else. The problem is that, many times, your survivability relies on you being on the move. You do not see survivalists just staying in one area. We would call this camping and not survivalism.

Why Choose where to Go?

You may think that it is wise to stay in one place, but setting up camp can be disastrous. Take the forest as an example. Living things beget other livings things and those living things may want to eat you. If you cook meat, which has a noticeable presence in the forest as the smell is great, then that smell is carried by the air. What will follow is that a meat eater will pick up the scent from miles away and move towards that location knowing there's a high chance that something containing meat is in that area. I know that the most common thoughts are that of predatory cats, wolves, and bears but you also have other animals like vultures, snakes, and potential zombies to worry about. You may think that last one was a joke, but it has been scientifically proven that rabies mixed with one of a few of the deadly viruses in the world can cause a virus that shows symptoms of zombification so it's only a matter of time before we start seeing combinations.

How to Choose where to Go?

Ironically, this is the easiest choice depending on your surroundings. If you are in an unknown land, the usual cause is that you've just survived an onslaught of some type of armed person or a plane crash. With an onslaught, they will often head off in the direction of their camp or the easiest place to navigate to where a good amount of their forces are. This really depends on where you are because if you're in Africa, you have a 50/50 chance that it will just be a straight up encampment or it could be a bazaar where there are militia hiding throughout the buildings. This is your choice, but I would head in the direction they went if I got to see where they went. This is because that direction will normally lead to more humans and if it is an encampment, I will be able to at least be able to find a road. That is the most important factor of surviving: finding a road. Roads lead to cities, which is how you can get back into society.

A plane crash is a different scenario, especially if you're on an island. The good news is that if there was a plane crash and you are stranded on an island, you want to stay on that island because rescue crew will be checking the islands near the crash site to see if there are survivors. The same is true of crashing in the middle of a country because rescue teams will be out there in either a couple of hours or days depending on how long it takes to recognize a problem. If, however, you are in a private aircraft then you have an issue. I don't mean to say you are rich and have a private plane of your own, but if you choose to hire a local flier to site see the area and it crashes then you have a problem. Unlike commercial airlines, local fliers do not have to check in with radio towers regularly. You do have a few things working in your favor here, though. Your pilot will have a map. It isn't "they might" it is a definite and most certain fact that they will have a map of the area you are in. They will use this to determine where they are in the scenario that they end up exactly as you ended up and any pilot that does not have a map on hand is a pilot you should not be trusting. They will also have some other useful things, like a first-aid kit and similar items. Using the map, you can easily find out where you need to go.

As you can see, nearly every situation where a commercial vehicle is involved the best thing you can do is stay in the area where the commercial vehicle is. This includes the fact that it may be burning. Just stay in the area and hopefully at a safe enough distance where a piece that's blown off will gut you in some area of your body.

Chapter 2 – Starter Mistakes

The first few hours that you are on the ground (or in the water) are the most important hours of your life, literally. There are four primary mistakes that beginning survivalists make during these crucial hours.

Searching For Food First

This is perhaps the worst possible mistake that you could make in your survival situation, but it wouldn't seem like this to a person who has never had to survive on the wilderness. Your first AND ONLY beginning objective in order to survive is to find a reasonably clean source of water. While it may be a bit longer in actual reality, I go with the phrase I learned from my father.

2 days, 2 weeks. It takes two days to die from lack of water, but it takes two weeks to die from a lack of food.

You are made up of water and your body needs a steady supply of it in order to keep running at its optimal output. Think of it like a computer. Sure, it's important to keep a computer fed with good equipment but it becomes pointless without electricity. This is why water is so vital to your body in comparison to food.

Drinking Unfiltered Water

The second worst mistake you could make in your survival situation is not to filter or boil your water. We've often heard that unclean water is bad for you and people tend to become desensitized when a warning is given out multiple times. Say you drink some unclean water that has a parasite that causes diarehea. Not only was the water you drank flushed out of your body, but, now, all the nutrients your food would have given you has been flushed out as well. On top of all of this, you wasted how much time in gathering those resources and then flushing them out of your body?

However, this is preventable by simply bringing the water to a boiling point. As soon as water reaches boiling point, most of the deadly contents inside will die off and the water will be relatively safe to drink. I say relatively because you could be ingesting the company waste products from up the stream and we've made movies about what could happen to you if you consume that.

Food Before Fire

Your first fire will not be for the food that you obtained but for the water you need to get inside of your body. Your first piece of food will likely not be meat, even though this is the most iconic image associated with surviving. You will undoubtedly want meat in the next couple of days, but the first thing you eat will likely be some type of plant and we'll get to the mistake that can happen with that. The plants you are likely going to eat are going to be rather close to you, unless you are in a desert in which case you are in the worst survival situation possible discounting natural disasters in some cases. Your first objectives are to get clean water in you and secure a safe place to sleep.

Why should you set up these two things first? You need water in order to keep functioning as a normal human being. You need a safe place to sleep to protect you from things like bugs, rain, and even heat. The sun can kill you. There is a reason why those who have been exposed to long hours in the sun have the most wrinkles when they grow old, but, beyond aesthetic features, the sun boils you. That's right, you literally cook underneath the light of the sun and if there's a lot of the sun then you are constantly losing water out of your body. This means you may reach a point where you cannot replenish what you lose, especially if getting to that water requires a great deal of effort.

Eating Any Plant

This one mistake is just as deadly as the previous mistakes, but this one will have a much more immediate effective. Let's take the classic Blueberry as an example. Unless you've picked blueberries for a portion of your life or you tend to longingly stare at blueberry pictures remembering a past time that is way too intimate then you likely don't have their exactly feel, look, and taste memorized. This can be deadly and confused with berries like Belladonna berries. Belladonna is commonly used in horror stories where the plot is based around someone being assassinated via poisoning. While the berries themselves are deadly, the leaves of this plant are worse. You can consume five berries and experience some horrible effects, but generally squeak out alive from the encounter. On the other hand, one leaf will kill you. It takes only one leaf for you to consume for this plant to kill you and it is not pretty when it does so. You'll have splitting headaches, lose your voice, have trouble breathing, and convulse until you die. As I said, this is not a pretty way to go and it can be very easy to confuse the two plants if you are not used to looking at blueberries for a long time. How can you prevent such issues?

Well, prevention is a heavy term but you can certainly prevent most from killing you. If you think you want to eat something, rub it on your arm and wait for around thirty minutes to see if it irritates your skin. Your skin is an organ so poisons will still affect it. Then, you put it on your tongue lightly, wait for just a minute, take it off, and then wait for a day to see if there are any ill effects. Your tongue will absorb a small amount of the poison contained within the plant, but usually not enough to kill you or make you feel absolutely horrible. Once you do that and you don't experience anything then you can eat it knowing that the chances of it being poisonous are significantly less than if you were to just pop it in your mouth as you pass by. Like I said, prevention is a heavy term but you can still mitigate a good portion of the ones that can cause harm. An example of something that can kill you if you put it on your tongue is Hemlock, but Hemlock is really easy to avoid since it just means you need to avoid white flowers. You can get more specific, but I doubt you're looking at flowers with thoughts of eating them. For your information, flowers are usually the ones that kill the most because many do not realize how harmful they can be.

Chapter 3 – Culinary Mistakes

Perhaps the oddest thing you could make a mistake on in the wild is cooking something wrong. I mean, at home it seems so simple. With meat, you just need to put it on the stove and it is magically delicious in just a few minutes of stirring or flipping. In the wild, the matter is entirely different because you no longer have a refrigerator or the FDA to protect you and they do a lot to protect your food (it's not their fault companies try to find away around the rules).

Cleaning Meat and Plants

The first thing you need to do with anything you plan to put in your body is clean it, but why? This is an interesting topic that many in the survivalist community just acknowledge as truth and move on. It's not that complicated, but let's go over it. You have good bacteria and bad bacteria. Good bacteria tends to thrive in organism's insides where the material is easy to gather and it is more beneficial to share something useful to gain something useful. Bad bacteria tends to thrive on the cusp of things, like in your mouth, near your butt, or in areas where the holes of your body are usually close to like the toilet or the toothbrush. Bad bacteria takes from you because that is how it is built to survive. It is the predator and parts of your body are its prey, but usually you have defenses against this.

There is one section of the body that does not have a good defense and this is your digestive track. Your digestive track relies on your mind to make good, sound decisions about what you put inside of your body. Therefore, while you may a minor amount of protection in the area of your oral cavity and your rectum, there are virtually not protections against bad bacteria once they get inside. The food is pushed down the pipe you share with the oxygen tube and dumped inside a vat of acid to be pushed through a long lining of tube that slowly absorbs the microbial crumbs of what you ate. Bad bacteria don't survive via endurance like we do. Instead, multiplying is how bad bacteria "survive" and since all it needs to multiply is itself and food, you digestive track has a hard time dealing with it: main vomiting or diarrhea. In other words, the only way your body can deal with bad bacteria once it is inside of you is to clean house in one of two doors and sometimes that isn't even effective enough.

Furthermore, bad bacteria tend to be buddies of viruses because the two of them penetrate other organisms in a very similar manner. Both have to get to an opening, both have to work through the digestive system most of the time, and the intestines is where they depart ways. Viruses are absorbed while bacteria is generally pushed out. Viruses do certain things to hide themselves from your bodies inner defenses so that it has time to replicate before fighting you on a massive scale.

Therefore, what kills bad bacteria and viruses that is not built inside of the body? Heat, ridiculous amounts of heat, and we're talking about heat that is triple to that of our own. Our body is a balmy 98.6 degrees with some variance. To kill bacteria and viruses, you need to be above 200 degrees as a minimum. This is why you need to cook all of your meats and plants, but why clean them?

Parasites. These run *wild* in the wild and their carcasses can still hold left over bad bacteria and/or viruses. That's right. Even if you boiled your meat and plants, the parasites could still give those deadly organisms that want to take your precious resources from you. With this in mind, it becomes imperative that you also clean your food, but how do you do that exactly? By using a second boiling. The first boiling will kill everything, but in the last moments of death a parasite can latch itself to the meat and can only be removed via movement of liquid. This is why boiling it a second time will remove any of the bacteria and yes, I am quite aware that this will make meat rather hard to eat. This will make the meat similar to jerky, which is actually a good thing in this scenario but it will still rot faster than actual jerky. The H2O of the water will be bouncing all over the place even though it is only the surface that looks like it is moving. Heat causes particles to move faster, which means the water inside of the container you are using is moving particularly fast at boiling point.

Cleaned Raw Meat Still Isn't Good

Say that you've killed most of the bacteria and, indeed, almost all the parasites because you're cleaning won't ever be as thorough as an industry lab. Would raw meat be edible at this point? Technically yes, but you would have to shove all of the meat in your mouth immediately after you have boiled it a second time. The issue here is in the rot that happens to meat. Do not think that there is nothing but a chemical cloud in the air you breathe. The parasites and bad bacteria use the air to travel and if you shine a bright light on a surface so that you can capture it with a slow motion camera, you will find there are a lot of objects flying around in the air. The stuff that floats around in the air is what carries the bacteria and it is still there in the wild, even more so as I doubt there is an Earth Cleaning Service you can call to clean a forest. Therefore, the moment the meat leaves the water is the moment the meat is at risk of regaining all the bad bacteria it just lost. The only way to prevent this is to cook the meat until all the blood is out of it. That's right, the only reason we cook meat in our homes before we eat it is to remove the blood from the meat and this removal of blood is what gives it that wonderful brownish black look. Ah, just talking about this makes my mouth water. Anyway, so when we cook the blood out we effectively eliminate the area where we will see bad bacteria germinate. After all, how can you land on something that is, effectively, a desert and try to absorb nutrients from it. There's nutrients inside of the meat, but it is much harder to get to.

Therefore, what actually happens is that the food has been cooked to the point where the bad bacteria do not have enough time to use the nutrients to multiply. This means your stomach won't have to fight as hard to kill the bad bacteria and win the day. This is the reason why you still cook your food even after it has been cleaned of all of the bad bacteria and parasites. You cook it so that the bad bacteria don't have enough nutrients to multiply and causes issues inside of your body.

Chapter 4 – Weapons Vs. Traps

Ironically, this is one choice that some people wouldn't see as a mistake but more of a circumstantial issue. However, this would be a very short chapter if all I said was that you should build traps before making a weapon.Therefore, let's go over what I mean and why I say making a weapon before making traps is a potentially bad mistake.

The Hours You Waste

When you think about survival, you often think about the time that you are awake and have the ability to do some hunting. The truth of the matter is that most of the easily catchable critters on this Earth tend to pop out at night. Night time is when most of the predators come out to see which animals left their sleeping spot unguarded and it is also the time when the animals who can't bare the hot sun come out of their hiding. Both of these animals tend to rely more on sound and smell than they do sight. After all, there's not a lot of light during the night time so relying on sight is not a particularly bright idea... gotta love the puns.

Most of your first day is comprised of finding and gathering water so that you can boil it for safe drinking. There's also the shelter that you need to build and the fire that the water will need you to build. Unless you woke up early in the morning, the odds are high that your first day started around noon and by the time you finished all that you needed to do on your first day you likely didn't have a lot of sunlight left on your hands. Therefore, you have a choice to make. Are you going to hopefully hunt down some meat at the risk of wasting a lot of calories or are you going to reserve most of those calories by making traps that can do the hunting for you while your body is shut down? For most survivalists, this decision is quite obvious but many still thinking of day hunting as their primary source of food.

Let's say you *did* make a weapon instead of making some traps. Traps can be made with weeds, rocks, and the very plants around you. Something like a spear requires a lot of work because you need to break the rock just right to get that sharp edge, you need to widdle out anything that could cause a splinter, and then you have to obtain the materials needed to keep the rock in place. There's a lot that goes into making a weapon and it usually takes a couple of hours to gather the materials and finally make it. Therefore, a trap that could be made in less than a half hour and then set in place in even less time is veritably more useful than a weapon that takes hours to make and will likely be useless until the next day.

The Potential Risks

The reason why many would consider this to be circumstantial has to do with the area you are in, the time of the day you started, and the ease of the two tasks. You might be trying to survive in an area where there's very little in the way of night creatures and building traps could potentially be a wasted effort that consumes time. Then you have the fact that if you started your survivalism in the morning then you would have enough time to make a weapon and hunt. Finally, if the materials are close at hand by natural *circumstance* then you will be able to form a weapon much faster.

Let's go through each of these and analyze their validity. The odds of you being in an area where you do not have a lot of night creatures is ludicrously low unless you are in a *rural* area, which means there are farms nearby. Anywhere there are humans, there's usually a lack of creatures all around. Animals do not like to go around things that make a lot of noise. One of the ways predators know when they are dealing with a massive animal or another predator is the iconic roar that the other animal lets loose. This is a threat to show how powerful they are because the more powerful the lungs means you have more oxygen flowing through your body and this also means you are likely to last longer in the fight. Predators want quick and easy to kill prey and will not usually take on massive enemies if they think it's going to be a long, drawn out battle. Therefore, animals tend to stay away from cities where the noise level is insane to them. Rural areas are where you begin to see the wolves and other fast predators because these areas produce a lot less noise. The further you branch out from the noise, the more likely you will find a lot more animals.

Another bit that is thrown at this has to be the fact that you could make a weapon if you decided to start your adventure in the morning. Alright, this one is based in diet theory by animals function like clocks and food is definitely one of them. Animals will hunt for food the most in the morning because they just got up and need to stock up for tomorrow as their body uses what it got the previous day. This is a continuous cycle that doesn't really break for any natural reason. The tricky part about when the animal hunts for food afterwards boils down to their stomach and their calorie needs for the day. Take the lion as an example. Provided the lion got in a good hunt in the morning, they usually eat their fill for about fifteen pounds but only as they need it. They may eat a lot more, up to even a hundred pounds, but then they won't eat again until a few days have passed. This is because they eat a lot so that they don't waste food and then they still don't eat until their body tells them they have balanced the calorie intake. This is where the problem lies because there could be predators or there could be no predators, but there are always herbivores. Now, herbivores are different only in the fact that they eat plants and they eat... constantly. If you see a deer stopped then you either also see them eating, watching children, or sleeping. There's not much else for them to do. To find them, you will have to start hunting around noon because that's when the most amount of tracks have been made but also with the shortest amount of closing distance between you and the herbivore. If the sun is not directly above you, your hunting window begins to close and it will be that much harder for you to track them down while you have sunlight. You also have to keep in mind that you have to double the time it takes you away from your safe area in order for you to be able to make it back to your safe area in time to start the fire again to cook the food. Like, no joke, it will take you a couple of hours to find the animal, hopefully you'll kill it, then it will take you x amount of time to get back, around 2 hours to fully cook it, and maybe 10 minutes to eat it. You will lose one-third of your day or more hunting down this meaty feast only to realize that all you need, in terms of meat, is a rabbit because it's the equivalent to a chicken breast.

Lastly, yes, if the materials are close at hand then you spend less time actually making the weapon and more time hunting, but as I mentioned in my last sentence you will spend one-third of your day grabbing way more meat than you actually need. If you want to go with the risk of missing out on meat altogether, because you may not even find prey or the prey may escape before you kill it, then by all means that is your choice.

How to avoid the need for either?

Fishing. For the first few days, you can fish using nothing but a net tied together by weeds, but the limitation to this is you have to have found a river that has a healthy amount of fish and a low-tide stream. You cannot effectively fish in a pond or a lake because you don't have the materials necessary (sometimes you do) in most cases to make a rod.

Conclusion

Welcome to the end of this book. We've gone over many of the common mistakes survivalists make that can endanger their lives. Hopefully, with this knowledge in your mind, you last much longer than they perhaps did.

FREE Bonus Reminder

If you have not grabbed it yet, please go ahead and download your special bonus report *"Preppers Survival Guide. Proven Tactics For Armed Incounters!"*

Simply Click the Button Below

OR **Go to This Page**

http://preppersliving.com/free

BONUS #2: More Free & Discounted Books & Products

Do you want to receive more Free/Discounted Books or Products?

We have a mailing list where we send out our new Books or Products when they go free or with a discount on Amazon. Click on the link below to sign up for Free & Discount Book & Product Promotions.

=> Sign Up for Free & Discount Book & Product Promotions <=

OR Go to this URL

http://zbit.ly/1WBb1Ek